AF572112

janis hansen

illustrated by wendy francisco

CROSSWAY BOOKS • WHEATON, ILLINOIS
A DIVISION OF GOOD NEWS PUBLISHERS

ROBIN ROAD PRODUCTIONS
SHERMAN OAKS, CALIFORNIA

Dedicated
to all the little children of the world

OTHER BIBLE ADVENTURE CLUB STORIES

Noah and the Incredible Flood

David and His Giant Battle

Jonah and His Amazing Voyage

Jesus: The Birthday of the King

Creation: God's Wonderful Gift

Published by Crossway Books, a division of Good News Publishers,
1300 Crescent Street, Wheaton, Illinois 60187

Illustrations: Wendy Francisco
First printing 2001
Printed in the United States of America

Library of Congress Cataloging-in-Publication Data
Hansen, Janis (Janis S.), 1942-
Creation : God's wonderful gift / Janis Hansen ; illustrated by Wendy Francisco.
p. cm. - (Bible Adventure club)
Summary: Illustrations and rhyming text describe God's creation of the world.
ISBN 1-58134-295-0 (alk. paper)
1. Creation-Juvenile literature. [1. Creation. 2. Bible stories-O.T.] I. Francisco, Wendy, ill. II. Title.
BS651 .H333 2001
222'.1109505-dc21 2001002272
CIP

15 14 13 12 11 10 09 08 07 06 05 04 03 02 01
15 14 13 12 11 10 9 8 7 6 5 4 3 2 1

A LETTER TO ADULTS

Welcome to the Bible Adventure on Creation!

We're sure the kids in your life will love the journey they're about to embark on. From the great storybook and audio-cassette to the fun-filled activity book and interactive CD-Rom, your young adventurers will discover the story of *Creation* in a new and exciting way. And the "Parents' Guide" will help you play a vital role in their experience.

Because what and how kids learn is important to us, we've had every element of *Creation: God's Wonderful Gift* reviewed by both a religious and an educational board of advisors. The content and vocabulary are appropriate for young children, and will help them develop reading and language skills, which are the cornerstones of education. Kids will also be able to expand and nourish their creativity as each Bible Adventure Club product challenges them to use their imagination. And most importantly, the knowledge they learn in these stories of God's Word will enhance their growing faith.

So begin with the great adventure stories of the Bible and start kids on a path that will enrich their lives in both faith and knowledge. And with you by their side, it'll be a fun-filled journey that you all will remember!

Annie, how did the world get like this with the sky and the sun and all the creatures and everything?"

"Well, Mikey, in the very beginning there was only God and nothing else. So ages and ages ago, God made this whole world and everything in it! Mom sang this song to me when I was small, and it explains it all."

"God said, 'Let there be light.'
And the light He called day,
And the dark was night."

"On the second day, God made sky,
With water below and the clouds up high."

"On the third day, God gave us land
With mountains and meadows and beaches of sand.
He made the flowers and trees with a wave of His hand,
And it was good."

"He made the sun and moon to give light.
He sprinkled planets and stars
Through the night—
Bright to light our way,
On the fourth day."

Puppy
Food

"God made this world,
From the mountains to the Milky Way.
He makes the time in every day,
Time to rest and time to work and play."

"Here, Goldie."

"He filled the sea with fishes and whales,
And birds made the sky come alive
On day number five."

"He made all the animals roaming the land;
Both man and woman came from His hand.
The sixth day was God's very busiest day,
I'm sure you will agree.
So the seventh day God decided to rest,
And the rest is history."

"God made the plants
And all the animals from A to Z.
Every person, every family—
God made Mom and Dad and you and me!"

"When we're done helping Mom, let's go to the beach!"

"He made the seals and the pelicans,
The dolphins and the whales."

*"Oh, oh, here comes a storm!
Quick, let's run home!"*

“He made the thunder and the cloudy skies,
The lightning and the hail.”

"God made the rainbows and the robins
And the hummingbirds and quail."

"Ooh, Mikey...look!"

“He made the crickets and the fireflies,
The spiders and the snails.”

“Come and get some ice cream, you two!”

"God made our friends
And our neighbors and our family.
He made the people far across the sea.
God made this beautiful world."

“God’s love shines down
On everybody, everywhere!”

"He made this world for us to share.
God made this beautiful world."